NATIONAL FOOTBALL LEAGUE
SUPER BOWL
INSIDE THE WORLD'S GREATEST GAME

NFL

by **Joe Layden**

SCHOLASTIC INC.

New York   Toronto   London   Auckland   Sydney
Mexico City   New Delhi   Hong Kong   Buenos Aires

IN ALL OF SPORTS, THERE IS NO EVENT MORE SPECTACULAR THAN THE SUPER BOWL.

Two football teams, featuring some of the greatest athletes in the world, locked in an epic battle for the right to call themselves champions. They've sweated and toiled for more than six months. The regular season is over. The playoffs, too. Where once there were 32 teams, now there are only two. And in a few hours, there will be only one. The Vince Lombardi Trophy will be held aloft. And the winners will feel like they are on top of the world.

Cowboys vs. Steelers,
Super Bowl XXX

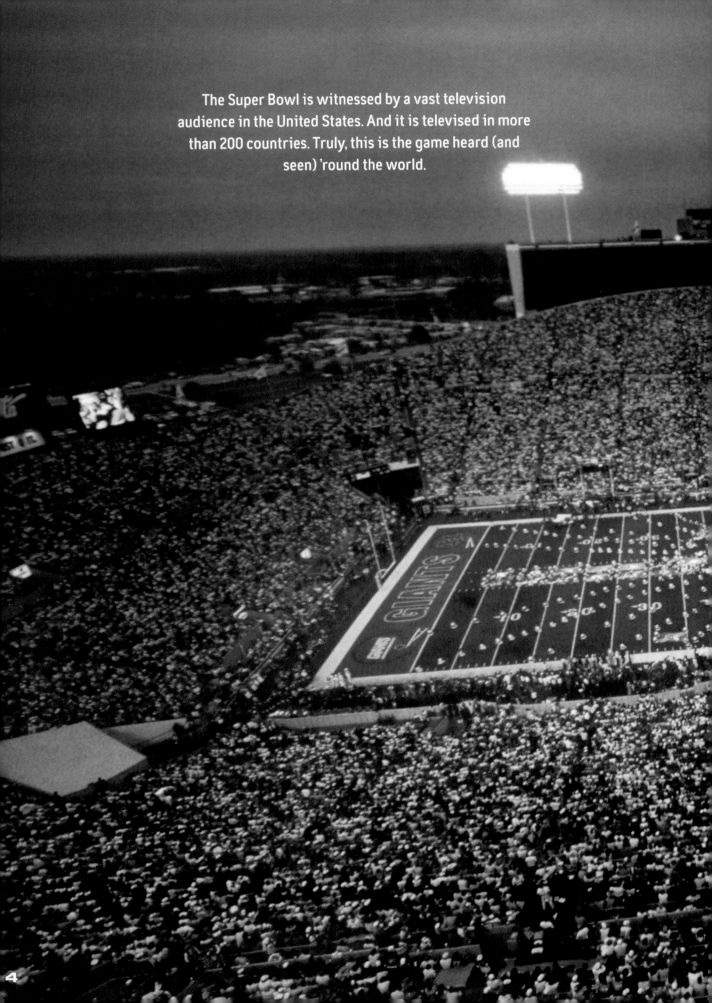

The Super Bowl is witnessed by a vast television audience in the United States. And it is televised in more than 200 countries. Truly, this is the game heard (and seen) 'round the world.

No wonder so many people consider Super Bowl Sunday to be an unofficial holiday. It's as if time stands still and everyone stops to enjoy the greatest single sporting event of them all!

Super Bowl XXV,
Tampa, Florida

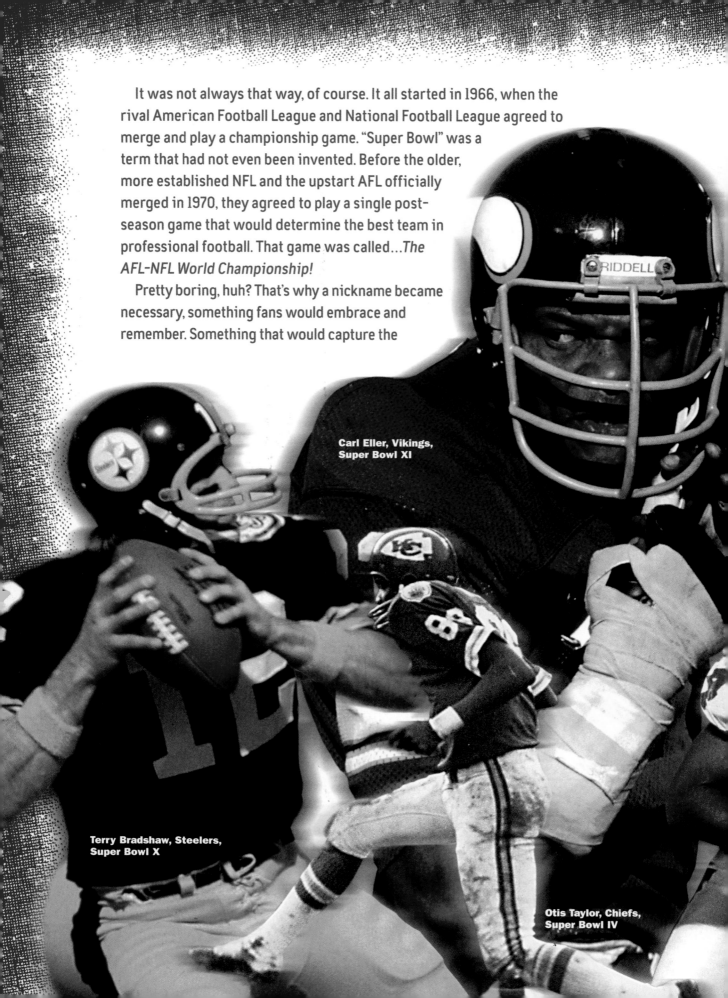

It was not always that way, of course. It all started in 1966, when the rival American Football League and National Football League agreed to merge and play a championship game. "Super Bowl" was a term that had not even been invented. Before the older, more established NFL and the upstart AFL officially merged in 1970, they agreed to play a single post-season game that would determine the best team in professional football. That game was called…*The AFL-NFL World Championship!*

Pretty boring, huh? That's why a nickname became necessary, something fans would embrace and remember. Something that would capture the

Carl Eller, Vikings,
Super Bowl XI

Terry Bradshaw, Steelers,
Super Bowl X

Otis Taylor, Chiefs,
Super Bowl IV

intensity and thrills of the game. Something that felt big and important. Something like…*The Super Bowl!*

Everyone seems to agree that the Super Bowl is worthy of its title. A game that did not even sell out in 1967 (there were nearly 40,000 empty seats in the Los Angeles Coliseum, site of the first Super Bowl) has become the hottest ticket in sports! Fans dream of getting a seat in the stadium, of being so close to the action that they can hear the pads smacking against each other.

Most of us settle for watching the game on television. But even in the comfort and quiet of our living rooms, the excitement comes through. As this book shows, no sporting event has produced more heart-pounding drama or more memorable moments than the Super Bowl. It rewards fans with some of the most sensational performances in the history of sports.

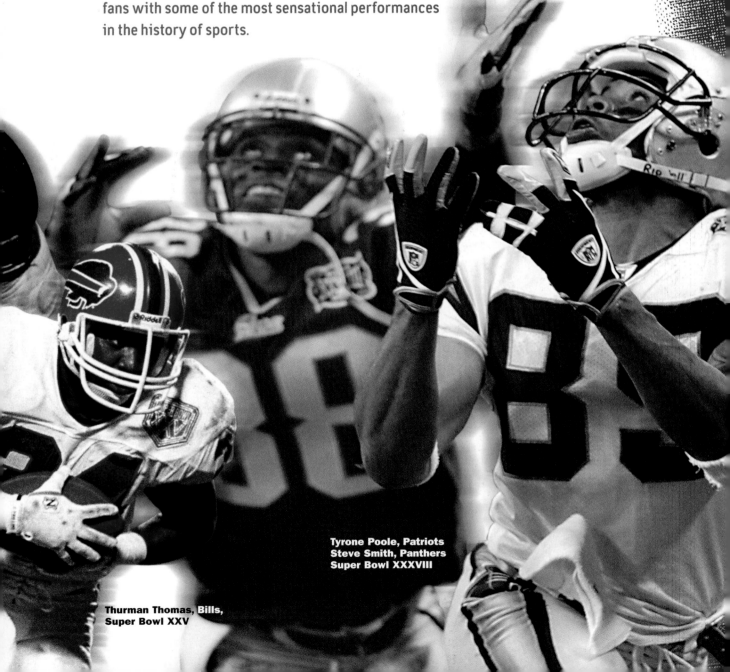

**Tyrone Poole, Patriots
Steve Smith, Panthers
Super Bowl XXXVIII**

**Thurman Thomas, Bills,
Super Bowl XXV**

THE WAITING IS THE HARDEST PART

In some ways, the build up of anticipation is also the best part.

Think about it. Imagine for just a few moments what it must be like to be a football player in the NFL. And not just any football player, but a member of the winning team as the clock winds down in either the AFC or NFC Championship Game. You are walking off the field, soaked in sweat, deliriously happy. This is what you've dreamed about since you were a kid. You are going to have an opportunity to play in the greatest sporting event of all: the Super Bowl! You are so excited that you could probably play right now! At this very minute. But you can't. Before the big game is the big build up. Two weeks of enormous anticipation and intense preparation. You are under the microscope now, and everyone is watching. Get used to it.

The greatest players know how to handle the pressure of the Super Bowl. Not just on the field, but off it, as well. The two-week gap between

Patriots' locker room, Super Bowl XXXVIII

Drew Bledsoe, Patriots, Super Bowl XXXVI

Jim McMahon, Bears, Super Bowl XX

Media Day, Super Bowl XXXVII

Joe Greene,
Steelers

the conference championships games and the Super Bowl is a mixed blessing for the teams. At this point in the season, after eighteen or nineteen games, muscles are sore and bones ache. Everyone is tired. So it is a relief to have some time to recover, to get back in shape for the test of a lifetime. Coaches like the break because it gives them time to study game film and figure out how to beat their opponent. But two weeks is a long time. Time for everyone to think and get nervous. Most players will tell you that by the time Super Bowl Sunday rolls around, they can't wait to get on the field!

There are plenty of distractions and obligations along the way. This is the Super Bowl, after all, and football fans want as much information as they can possibly get. There is a feeding frenzy among the journalists who cover the game and the events leading up to it. If you want to get a real sense of the magnitude of The Super Bowl, consider this: the NFL distributes official media credentials to close to 4,000 representatives from around the world! These reporters send stories back to hundreds of millions of fans in nearly 200 countries. To help the media meet its obligations, players spend several hours conducting

NFL great Y.A. Tittle makes the coin toss, Super Bowl XXXVIII

interviews during Super Bowl week. It can be tiring, and it takes time, but it's a valuable part of the job.

The days creep by, the pressure builds, but soon enough it is Sunday afternoon. Finally…time to play football! The game-day routine is familiar and comforting. It helps ease some of the tension. The players arrive several hours before kickoff. They meet with coaches and trainers. They go through the ritual of taping their ankles and wrists, and putting on their uniforms. As the sun fades and game-time draws near, nervousness is replaced by excitement! The players hit the field through a tunnel of teammates and cheerleaders as the crowd roars its approval. A performance of the National Anthem is punctuated with a flyover by U.S. military jets.

It's almost game time!

The captains of both teams walk to the middle of the field. A coin is tossed. The referee announces which team will receive the kickoff. There are handshakes and quiet greetings. And then, for just a moment, as the teams line up, there is silence. The kicker approaches the ball. The crowd rises and cheers with all its might.

The game has begun!

Jamal Anderson, Falcons, Super Bowl XXXIII

Pre-game ceremony,
Super Bowl XXXVIII

Super Bowl VI
January 16, 1972
Dallas Cowboys 24
Miami Dolphins 3
Behind a stingy defense and the athleticism of quarterback Roger Staubach, who throws two touchdown passes, Dallas wins its first Super Bowl title.

MVP: Roger Staubach, QB, Cowboys

Super Bowl VII
January 14, 1973
Miami Dolphins 14
Washington Redskins 7
Jim Kiick scores one touchdown and Bob Griese throws a TD pass to Howard Twilley as the Dolphins score twice in the first half and then hold on for the victory. They finish the year with a perfect 17–0 record.

MVP: Jake Scott, S, Dolphins

Super Bowl VIII
January 13, 1974
Miami Dolphins 24
Minnesota Vikings 7
Call it a dynasty! Behind the backfield of Jim Kiick and Larry Csonka, the Dolphins use a devastating running attack to beat the Vikings and repeat as world champions.

MVP: Larry Csonka, RB, Dolphins

Super Bowl IX
January 12, 1975
Pittsburgh Steelers 16
Minnesota Vikings 6
The Steel Curtain falls on the Vikings, who manage to gain only 17 yards rushing the entire game! Franco Harris rushes for 158 yards and one TD to lead the Steelers.

MVP: Franco Harris, RB, Steelers

Super Bowl X
January 18, 1976
Pittsburgh Steelers 21
Dallas Cowboys 17
Lynn Swann's spectacular 64-yard touchdown reception on a pass from Terry Bradshaw sparks the Steelers to a second championship. It also goes down in history as one of the Super Bowl's greatest plays.
MVP: Lynn Swann, WR, Steelers

Super Bowl XI
January 9, 1977
Oakland Raiders 32
Minnesota Vikings 14
The Raiders featured a balanced offensive attack, led by running back Clarence Davis and wide receiver Fred Biletnikoff, proving themselves nearly unstoppable as they handed the Vikings yet another bitter defeat.
MVP: Fred Biletnikoff, WR, Raiders

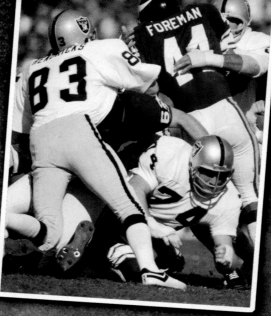

Super Bowl XII
January 15, 1978
Dallas Cowboys 27
Denver Broncos 10
A crushing defense forces a record eight turnovers as the Cowboys win their second Super Bowl. The outcome is never in doubt as Dallas takes a 13-0 halftime lead and a 21-0 advantage early in the third quarter.
MVPs: Randy White, DT, Cowboys; Harvey Martin, DE, Cowboys

LARRY CSONKA
Miami Dolphins

Some guys just look like football players. Take Larry Csonka, for example. With a thicket of a mustache sprouting beneath a battered nose, and an obvious fondness for running over defenders, Csonka was a man built to play the game. There was nothing pretty about Csonka. He was a bull in shoulder pads, always charging with his head down, and using two hands to cradle the ball. For him, fumbling was not an option. He was the perfect leader for a team that was all business, and never flashy. Csonka helped the Dolphins to an undefeated season in 1972, including a 14-7 victory over the Washington Redskins in Super Bowl VII. The next year, when the Dolphins repeated as champions, Csonka was even better. He rushed for a then-Super Bowl record 145 yards, scored two touchdowns and was named MVP as Miami beat the Minnesota Vikings, 24-7.

Super Bowl XIII

January 21, 1979
Pittsburgh Steelers 35
Dallas Cowboys 31
The Steelers lock up their third Super Bowl title thanks largely to the performance of quarterback Terry Bradshaw, who completes 17 of 30 passes for 318 yards and four touchdowns.

MVP: Terry Bradshaw, QB, Steelers

Super Bowl XIV

January 20, 1980
Pittsburgh Steelers 31
Los Angeles Rams 19
There is no stopping Pittsburgh! Or Terry Bradshaw. Once again the QB has a great game (14 of 21 for 309 yards and two TDs) as coach Chuck Noll's Steelers successfully defend their title.

MVP: Terry Bradshaw, QB, Steelers

Super Bowl XV

January 25, 1981
Oakland Raiders 27
Philadelphia Eagles 10
Jim Plunkett, a veteran backup quarterback just one year earlier, throws three touchdown passes as the Raiders become the first wild card team to win the Super Bowl.

MVP: Jim Plunkett, QB, Raiders

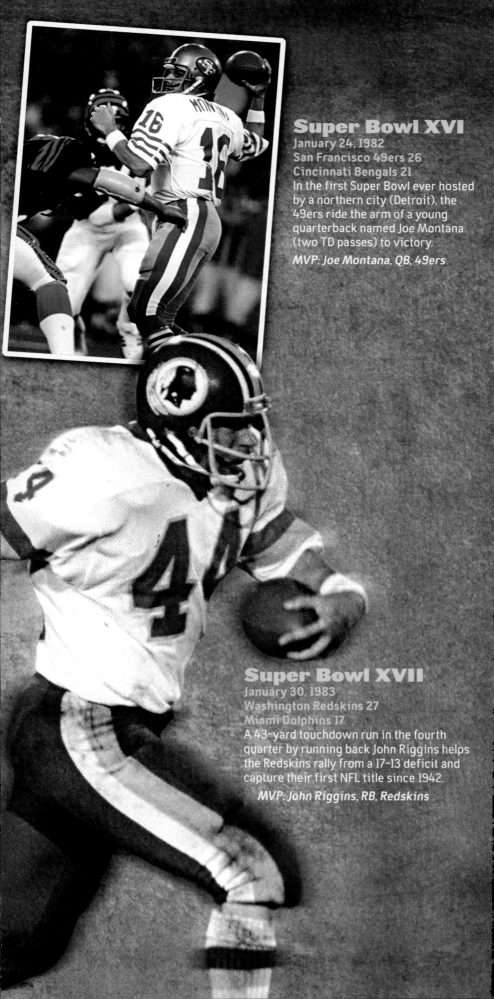

Super Bowl XVI

January 24, 1982
San Francisco 49ers 26
Cincinnati Bengals 21
In the first Super Bowl ever hosted by a northern city (Detroit), the 49ers ride the arm of a young quarterback named Joe Montana (two TD passes) to victory.

MVP: Joe Montana, QB, 49ers

Super Bowl XVII

January 30, 1983
Washington Redskins 27
Miami Dolphins 17
A 43-yard touchdown run in the fourth quarter by running back John Riggins helps the Redskins rally from a 17-13 deficit and capture their first NFL title since 1942.

MVP: John Riggins, RB, Redskins

JOE GREENE

Pittsburgh Steelers

At the heart of the famous "Steel Curtain" defense of the Pittsburgh Steelers was a 6-foot-4, 260-pound defensive lineman known as Mean Joe Greene. Of course, it was only opponents who saw him that way. To teammates he was a hero. As one of them once said, "Having Joe on your side is like having a big brother around when the bullies are coming to fight you." Despite his size and reputation for toughness, it was speed that was actually Greene's greatest asset. He was one of the fastest and most agile players of his era. When the ball was snapped, he would pounce into the backfield, his massive body little more than a blur, and quickly smother the quarterback or ball carrier. Led by Greene, a Hall of Famer, and the Steel Curtain, Pittsburgh built one of the greatest dynasties in sports, winning four Super Bowls in six years during the 1970s.

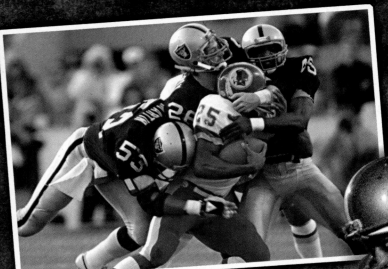

Super Bowl XVIII
January 2, 1984
Los Angeles Raiders 38
Washington Redskins 9
Marcus Allen rushes for 191 yards on 20 carries, including a dazzling 74-yard touchdown run in the third quarter as the Raiders roll to victory.
MVP: Marcus Allen, RB, Raiders

Super Bowl XIX
January 20, 1985
San Francisco 49ers 38
Miami Dolphins 16
Joe Montana proves he is not only a great passer, but an exceptional all-around athlete. San Francisco's quarterback throws for 331 yards and three touchdowns. He also rushes for 59 yards and one TD.
MVP: Joe Montana, QB, 49ers

Super Bowl XX
January 26, 1986
Chicago Bears 46
New England Patriots 10
The Chicago Bears take their Super Bowl Shuffle to New Orleans and defeat the New England Patriots. Although the Bears score 46 points, it's really a victory for the defense, which holds New England to just seven rushing yards.
MVP: Richard Dent, DE, Bears

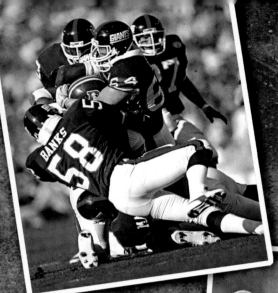

Super Bowl XXI

January 25, 1987
New York Giants 39
Denver Broncos 20

The Giants make their first Super Bowl appearance a memorable one, thanks primarily to a flawless performance by quarterback Phil Simms, who completes 22 of 25 passes (a Super Bowl record) for 268 yards and three touchdowns.

MVP: Phil Simms, QB, Giants

PHIL SIMMS

New York Giants

Phil Simms suffered through some lean seasons with the Giants during his early years in the NFL. But in 1986 he led one of the league's oldest and proudest franchises back to greatness as the Giants won their first title since 1956. Simms saved his greatest game for the world's biggest stage— Super Bowl XXI. On this pressure-packed day, the gritty Simms—noted more for his leadership than his accuracy—responded by completing pass after pass. By the end of the game, Simms had completed 22 of 25 passes for 268 yards, including three touchdown passes. It was the highest percentage of completions by any quarterback in Super Bowl history. The Giants rolled to 39-20 victory.

Super Bowl XXII

January 31, 1988
Washington Redskins 42
Denver Broncos 10

An offensive explosion (five touchdowns in just 18 plays!) in the second quarter allows the Redskins to erase a 10-0 deficit and cruise to their second Super Bowl title.

MVP: Doug Williams, QB, Redskins

Super Bowl XXIII

January 22, 1989
San Francisco 49ers 20
Cincinnati Bengals 16

The 49ers' third title features a heart-stopping finish in which Joe Montana directs a 92-yard scoring drive and fires a game-winning TD pass to John Taylor with 34 seconds remaining.

MVP: Jerry Rice, WR, 49ers

Super Bowl XXIV
January 28, 1990
San Francisco 49ers 55
Denver Broncos 10
Joe Montana adds to his legacy with another Super Bowl ring. This time he throws for 297 yards and five touchdowns as the 49ers set a Super Bowl record for points scored.

MVP: Joe Montana, QB, 49ers

Super Bowl XXV
January 27, 1991
New York Giants 20
Buffalo Bills 19
In one of the most exciting Super Bowl games ever played, the Giants hang on for a one-point victory after Scott Norwood's 47-yard field goal attempt in the final seconds sails wide to the right.

MVP: Ottis Anderson, RB, Giants

Super Bowl XXVI

January 26, 1992
Washington Redskins 37
Buffalo Bills 24

A little-known quarterback named Mark Rypien plays the game of his life as the Redskins win their third title. Rypien completes 18 of 33 passes, including seven to Art Monk, one of the game's all-time leading receivers.

MVP: Mark Rypien, QB, Redskins

JERRY RICE

San Francisco 49ers

Jerry Rice has always made the game look easy. But don't let that fool you. The truth is that Rice is a fiercely dedicated athlete who works harder than just about anyone who has ever played the game. His off-season workouts are legendary. Rice lifts weights for hours and runs sprints until he is ready to collapse. By the time the season begins, he is always in tremendous condition. Rice's career has been filled with great accomplishments, including four Super Bowl titles. The most memorable came in Super Bowl XXIII, when the 49ers beat the Cincinnati Bengals, 20-16. A lot of people remember this game because it featured a last-second touchdown pass from quarterback Joe Montana to wide receiver John Taylor. But Rice was the real hero, and the game's MVP. He caught 11 passes for 215 yards. Both still stand as Super Bowl records.

Super Bowl XXVII

January 31, 1993
Dallas Cowboys 52
Buffalo Bills 17

Four years after being selected first in the NFL draft, Troy Aikman lives up to his reputation. The QB throws four touchdown passes as the Cowboys roll.

MVP: Troy Aikman, QB, Cowboys

Super Bowl XXVIII

January 30, 1994
Dallas Cowboys 30
Buffalo Bills 13

What a difference a year makes? Not really. The Bills and Cowboys meet again, and the result is another victory for Dallas. Emmitt Smith leads the way with 132 yards rushing and two touchdowns.

MVP: Emmitt Smith, RB, Cowboys

Super Bowl XXIX

January 29, 1995
San Francisco 49ers 49
San Diego Chargers 26
Steve Young takes over as quarterback for San Francisco and has one of the greatest games in Super Bowl history. He throws a record six touchdowns as the 49ers become the first team to win five Super Bowls.

MVP: Steve Young, QB, 49ers

Super Bowl XXX

January 28, 1996
Dallas Cowboys 27
Pittsburgh Steelers 17
Larry Brown's two interceptions in the second half lead to two touchdowns and help the Cowboys break open a close game and pull away from the Steelers.

MVP: Larry Brown, DB, Cowboys

Super Bowl XXXI

January 26, 1997
Green Bay Packers 35
New England Patriots 21
The Pack is back! Brett Favre throws two touchdown passes and runs for another touchdown as Green Bay wins its first Super Bowl in 29 years.

MVP: Desmond Howard, KR, Packers

Super Bowl XXXII

January 25, 1998
Denver Broncos 31
Green Bay Packers 24

The Broncos, losers in four previous Super Bowls, finally get their rings. The winning touchdown comes on a one-yard run by Terrell Davis with 1:45 left in the game.

MVP: Terrell Davis, RB, Broncos

Super Bowl XXXIII

January 31, 1999
Denver Broncos 34
Atlanta Falcons 19

Quarterback John Elway, playing in his final game, throws for 336 yards as the Broncos become the first AFC team since the Pittsburgh Steelers to win back-to-back Super Bowls.

MVP: John Elway, QB, Broncos

Super Bowl XXXIV

January 30, 2000
St. Louis Rams 23
Tennessee Titans 16

Kurt Warner throws for 414 yards and two touchdowns, but it is the defense that saves the day for the Rams, as Mike Jones tackles Tennessee receiver Kevin Dyson at the one-yard line on the game's final play.

MVP: Kurt Warner, QB, Rams

Super Bowl XXXV

January 28, 2001
Baltimore Ravens 34
New York Giants 7

In their first Super Bowl appearance, the Ravens, led by linebacker Ray Lewis, force five turnovers and limit the Giants to just 152 yards of total offense.

MVP: Ray Lewis, LB, Ravens

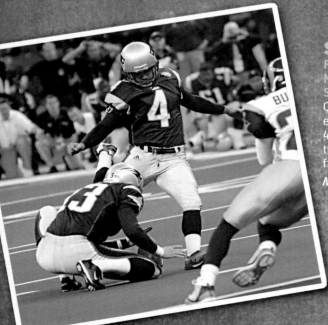

Super Bowl XXXVI

February 3, 2002
New England Patriots 20
St. Louis Rams 17

Quarterback Tom Brady leads a game-ending drive and Adam Vinatieri kicks a 48-yard field goal as time expires to give the Patriots a dramatic victory and their first Super Bowl title.

MVP: Tom Brady, QB, Patriots

Super Bowl XXXVII

January 26, 2003
Tampa Bay Buccaneers 48
Oakland Raiders 21

At 39 years of age, the fiercely competitive Jon Gruden becomes the youngest coach to win a Super Bowl ring. Defense gets the job done for the Bucs, who return three interceptions for touchdowns!

MVP: Dexter Jackson, S, Bucs

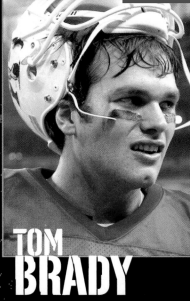

TOM BRADY

New England Patriots

At age 24, Tom Brady faced the biggest football game of his life, Super Bowl XXXVI. So half an hour before the game, he lay on the locker-room floor—and napped! Tom awoke feeling calm and confident. Then he led the Patriots to Super Bowl victory, 20-17 over the St. Louis Rams, and brought home a nifty piece of hardware, the MVP trophy. Tom became an instant star, the youngest quarterback to win the Super Bowl!

As if that wasn't enough, two years later Tom pulled off the same feat. Another Super Bowl victory, another MVP. Ho-hum. Tom achieves his remarkable results with cool efficiency, just quietly winning games. Perhaps for that reason, Brady was underrated by many so-called experts. But those days are gone. When you have two Super Bowl rings and a nice trophy collection, well, even the naysayers tend to stand up and take notice.

Super Bowl XXXVIII

February 1, 2004
New England Patriots 32
Carolina Panthers 29

Talk about a familiar feeling! For the second time in three years, Adam Vinatieri kicked a field goal to save the day for the Patriots. This one came from 41 yards out with only four seconds remaining in a wild game featuring the highest-scoring fourth-quarter in Super Bowl history.

MVP: Tom Brady, QB, Patriots

Broadway Joe

New York Jets quarterback Joe Namath had brazenly (and some people thought foolishly) predicted that his team would upset the heavily favored NFL champion Baltimore Colts in Super Bowl III. And they did, by a score of 16-7. As the game came to an end, Namath, wearing his trademark white shoes, jogged off the field with a smile on his face and an index finger raised in the air. It was never in doubt!

The Rookie

First-year kicker Jim O'Brien of the Baltimore Colts stood on the field in the final seconds of Super Bowl V. Like many kickers faced with the pressure of nailing a game-winning field goal, he tried to pull up a few blades of grass to test the wind in Miami's Orange Bowl. There was just one problem: the field was made of artificial turf! O'Brien overcame his jitters and drilled a 32-yard field goal with five seconds remaining to give the Colts a 16-13 victory over the Dallas Cowboys.

The
Acrobat

There have been a lot of great plays in the Super Bowl, but none more acrobatic than Lynn Swann's reception of a pass from Pittsburgh Steelers quarterback Terry Bradshaw in Super Bowl X. Swann leaped incredibly high over Dallas Cowboys defensive back Mark Washington to get his hands on the pass. Even though he bobbled the ball while falling and hit the ground hard, Swann never lost his concentration. That remarkable 53-yard play helped the Steelers gain a 21-17 victory.

The Fridge

The 1986 Chicago Bears were a team filled with larger-than-life personalities. But none was larger than William "The Refrigerator" Perry, a 310-pound defensive lineman with a gap-toothed smile nearly as wide as his belly. The Fridge was one of the league's most popular players during the Bears' championship season. And he capped it all off by lining up at running back and rumbling in for a one-yard touchdown run in Chicago's 46-10 win over the New England Patriots in Super Bowl XX.

Taylor Made

It is hard to say what was more impressive: the game-winning pass from Joe Montana to John Taylor with 34 seconds left in Super Bowl XXIII, or the celebration that followed. Taylor was one of the game's most gifted athletes. His reception capped a 92-yard drive and gave the 49ers a 20-16 victory over the Cincinnati Bengals. As the crowd went wild, Taylor ran to the back of the end zone and leaped toward the sky, holding the ball aloft. It seemed for a moment as though he might never come down.

One Tough QB

After losing his first three Super Bowls, Denver Broncos quarterback John Elway was not about to lose a fourth. He did everything in his power to carry the Broncos to victory in Super Bowl XXXII, including risking his body. On a memorable third-down play from the Green Bay Packers' 12-yard line, Elway scrambled out of the pocket and leaped for the first down marker. He crashed into two defenders and was tossed into the air, spinning like a helicopter, but somehow managed to get the first down. Afterward, he jumped to his feet and waved a clenched fist at his teammates. And the Broncos went on to upset the Packers.

The Longest Yard

So close, and yet so far. One yard, to be precise. That is all that stood between the Tennessee Titans and possible victory in Super Bowl XXXIV. On the final play of the game, St. Louis Rams linebacker Mike Jones made the play of a lifetime, stopping Titans receiver Kevin Dyson at the one yard line to preserve a 23-16 victory and give the Rams their first Super Bowl title.

SPECTACULAR PERFORMANCES
SINGLE-GAME SUPER BOWL RECORDS

Most Touchdowns
3   Roger Craig, S.F., XIX
    Jerry Rice, S.F., XXIV
    Ricky Watters, S.F., XXIX
    Terrell Davis, Den., XXXII

Most Field Goals
4   Don Chandler, G.B., II
    Ray Wersching, S.F., XVI

Longest Field Goal
54 Steve Christie, Buff., XXVIII

Most Rushing Yards Gained
204   Timmy Smith, Wash., XXII
191   Marcus Allen, L.A., XVIII
166   John Riggins, Wash., XVII

Longest Run from Scrimmage
74 Marcus Allen, L.A., XVIII

Rushing Touchdowns, Game
3   Terrell Davis, Den., XXXII

Highest Completion Percentage (20 attempts)
88.0   Phil Simms, N.Y.G., XXI
75.9   Joe Montana, S.F., XXIV
73.5   Ken Anderson, Cin., XVI

Passing Yards Gained
414   Kurt Warner, St.L., XXXIV
365   Kurt Warner, St.L., XXXVI
357   Joe Montana, S.F., XXIII

Longest Pass Completion
81 Brett Favre (to Antonio Freeman), G.B., XXXI

Most Touchdown Passes
6   Steve Young, S.F., XXIX

Most Receptions
11   Dan Ross, Cin., XVI
     Jerry Rice, S.F., XXIII

Receiving Yards Gained
215   Jerry Rice, S.F., XXIII
193   Ricky Sanders, Wash., XXII
162   Isaac Bruce, St.L., XXXIV

Sacks
3.0   Reggie White, G.B., XXXI

Jerry Rice, 49ers, Super Bowl XXIX